How Much More

Written by Alice Wilson-Sharp

Illustrated by Kristoffer and Amy Friesen

Kingdom Publishers

Copyright© Alice Wilson-Sharp 2025

All rights reserved. No part of this book may be reproduced in any form by photocopying or any electronic or mechanical means, including information storage or retrieval systems, without permission in writing from both the copyright owner and the publisher of the book. The right of Alice Wilson-Sharp to be identified as the author of this work has been asserted by her in accordance with the Copyright, Designs, and Patents Act 1988 and any subsequent amendments thereto.

A catalogue record for this book is available from the British Library.

ISBN: 978-1-916801-45-5

1st Edition 2025 by Kingdom Publishers, London, UK.

You can purchase copies of this book from any leading bookstore or at:
www.kingdompublishers.co.uk

For Daisy

This book is given to

....

With love from

....

Sometimes,
I have a worry day …
An 'everything in a hurry' day,
An 'I'm just not feeling myself' day,
An 'I'm going to hide away' day.

But I can press 'stop' inside my head;
Tell the worry thoughts to 'go' instead.
They are not allowed to stay in me,
For Jesus is always here with me.

He made the birds up in the sky,
Gliding and racing way up high.

He made hovering hummingbirds,

And long-legged running birds!

Sleek and speedy diving birds,

See-in-the-dark night-time birds,

Early morning singing birds,

And water-loving wading birds.

He made the flowers all around,

With roots growing deep into the ground.

They do not need to work or run,

    For God gave them soil and rain and sun.

God made seeds – they're miracles all –
From these may grow sunflowers tall ...

Or fresh and tasty veggies...

Or sweet and juicy berries ...

Or mighty trees in forests!
From the smallest to the greatest,
All these grow because of God's care.
Imagine if they were not there!

God made and feeds and loves all these.
But how much more does He love me!

In the darkness of the night,

    God's work is still within our sight.

He made the glittering stars,

    And gave them each a home afar.

He made enormous planets, too,
And shining comets flying through.
He made all this, just for us,
So many things that are glorious!

God made and guides and loves all these.
But how much more does He love me!

So I can take my worries one by one,
  And give them to God when the day is done.
He can sort out all that I face
  And help me put fear in its place.

He takes away the yuckiness,
The tears and all the grumpiness.
And I can sleep in perfect rest,
For God's with me and I am blessed.

My God made birds
and flowers and stars,
Big and small and near and far.
He helps and knows and loves all these ...
But how much more does He love me!

Bedtime Prayer

Dear God,

Thank You for all the good things that have happened today. (You might like to talk about some).

Thank You for loving me more than the birds and the flowers and the stars.

I give You all the things that have made me sad or worried today and leave them with You to sort out.

I pray for a good sleep,

in Jesus' name. Amen.

www.ingramcontent.com/pod-product-compliance
Lightning Source LLC
Chambersburg PA
CBHW041154070526
44584CB00004B/310